NEW ADVENTURES

PARANORMAL DOOR PUBLISHING
29 Anzac Road, Morningside, Whangarei 0110,
New Zealand. admin@pdpublisher.com
www.pdpublisher.com
This book is an original publication of Paranormal Door Publishing.
NEW ADVENTURES © JUNE 2018
1ST Edition

ISBN-13:978-1721575879
ISBN-10:1721575871

Month

Year

Motivational quote / Monthly Goal

Month/Year			
Monday	**Tuesday**	**Wednesday**	**Thursday**
—	—	—	—
—	—	—	—
—	—	—	—
—	—	—	—
—	—	—	—

Motivation:			
Friday	**Saturday**	**Sunday**	**Notes**
—	—	—	—
—	—	—	—
—	—	—	—
—	—	—	—

Month/Year	
Important Dates	**Tasks**
1	
2	
3	
4	
5	
6	
7	
8	
9	
10	
11	
12	
13	
14	
15	
16	
17	
18	
19	
20	
21	
22	
23	
24	
25	
26	
27	
28	
29	
30	
31	

Month /Year			
Monday	**Tuesday**	**Wednesday**	**Thursday**
1	1	1	1
2	2	2	2
3	3	3	3
4	4	4	4
5	5	5	5
Notes	Notes	Notes	Notes

Weekly motivation or goal:

Friday	Saturday	Sunday	Notes
1	1	1	
2	2	2	
3	3	3	
4	4	4	
5	5	5	
Notes	**Notes**	**Notes**	

Month /Year			
Monday	**Tuesday**	**Wednesday**	**Thursday**
1	1	1	1
2	2	2	2
3	3	3	3
4	4	4	4
5	5	5	5
Notes	Notes	Notes	Notes

Weekly motivation or goal:			
Friday	**Saturday**	**Sunday**	**Notes**
1	1	1	
2	2	2	
3	3	3	
4	4	4	
5	5	5	
Notes	**Notes**	**Notes**	

Month /Year			
Monday	**Tuesday**	**Wednesday**	**Thursday**
1	1	1	1
2	2	2	2
3	3	3	3
4	4	4	4
5	5	5	5
Notes	**Notes**	**Notes**	**Notes**

Weekly motivation or goal:

Friday	Saturday	Sunday	Notes
1	1	1	
2	2	2	
3	3	3	
4	4	4	
5	5	5	
Notes	Notes	Notes	

Month /Year			
Monday	**Tuesday**	**Wednesday**	**Thursday**
1	1	1	1
2	2	2	2
3	3	3	3
4	4	4	4
5	5	5	5
Notes	Notes	Notes	Notes

Weekly motivation or goal:

Friday	Saturday	Sunday	Notes
1	1	1	
2	2	2	
3	3	3	
4	4	4	
5	5	5	
Notes	**Notes**	**Notes**	

Month /Year			
Monday	**Tuesday**	**Wednesday**	**Thursday**
1	1	1	1
2	2	2	2
3	3	3	3
4	4	4	4
5	5	5	5
Notes	**Notes**	**Notes**	**Notes**

Weekly motivation or goal:

Friday	Saturday	Sunday	Notes
1	1	1	
2	2	2	
3	3	3	
4	4	4	
5	5	5	
Notes	Notes	Notes	

Month

Year

Motivational quote / Monthly Goal

Month/Year			
Monday	**Tuesday**	**Wednesday**	**Thursday**
—	—	—	—
—	—	—	—
—	—	—	—
—	—	—	—
—	—	—	—

Motivation:			
Friday	**Saturday**	**Sunday**	**Notes**
—	—	—	—
—	—	—	—
—	—	—	—
—	—	—	—

Month/Year	
Important Dates	**Tasks**
1	
2	
3	
4	
5	
6	
7	
8	
9	
10	
11	
12	
13	
14	
15	
16	
17	
18	
19	
20	
21	
22	
23	
24	
25	
26	
27	
28	
29	
30	
31	

Month /Year			
Monday	Tuesday	Wednesday	Thursday
1	1	1	1
2	2	2	2
3	3	3	3
4	4	4	4
5	5	5	5
Notes	Notes	Notes	Notes

Weekly motivation or goal:

Friday	Saturday	Sunday	Notes
1	1	1	
2	2	2	
3	3	3	
4	4	4	
5	5	5	
Notes	**Notes**	**Notes**	

Month /Year			
Monday	**Tuesday**	**Wednesday**	**Thursday**
1	1	1	1
2	2	2	2
3	3	3	3
4	4	4	4
5	5	5	5
Notes	**Notes**	**Notes**	**Notes**

Weekly motivation or goal:			
Friday	**Saturday**	**Sunday**	**Notes**
1	1	1	
2	2	2	
3	3	3	
4	4	4	
5	5	5	
Notes	**Notes**	**Notes**	

Month /Year			
Monday	**Tuesday**	**Wednesday**	**Thursday**
1	1	1	1
2	2	2	2
3	3	3	3
4	4	4	4
5	5	5	5
Notes	**Notes**	**Notes**	**Notes**

Weekly motivation or goal:

Friday	Saturday	Sunday	Notes
1	1	1	
2	2	2	
3	3	3	
4	4	4	
5	5	5	
Notes	Notes	Notes	

Month /Year			
Monday	**Tuesday**	**Wednesday**	**Thursday**
1	1	1	1
2	2	2	2
3	3	3	3
4	4	4	4
5	5	5	5
Notes	Notes	Notes	Notes

Weekly motivation or goal:

Friday	Saturday	Sunday	Notes
1	1	1	
2	2	2	
3	3	3	
4	4	4	
5	5	5	
Notes	**Notes**	**Notes**	

Month /Year

Monday	Tuesday	Wednesday	Thursday
1	1	1	1
2	2	2	2
3	3	3	3
4	4	4	4
5	5	5	5
Notes	Notes	Notes	Notes

Weekly motivation or goal:

Friday	Saturday	Sunday	Notes
1	1	1	
2	2	2	
3	3	3	
4	4	4	
5	5	5	
Notes	**Notes**	**Notes**	

Month

Year

Motivational quote / Monthly Goal

Month/Year			
Monday	**Tuesday**	**Wednesday**	**Thursday**
—	—	—	—
—	—	—	—
—	—	—	—
—	—	—	—
—	—	—	—

Motivation:			
Friday	**Saturday**	**Sunday**	**Notes**
—	—	—	—
—	—	—	—
—	—	—	—
—	—	—	—

Month/Year	
Important Dates	**Tasks**
1	
2	
3	
4	
5	
6	
7	
8	
9	
10	
11	
12	
13	
14	
15	
16	
17	
18	
19	
20	
21	
22	
23	
24	
25	
26	
27	
28	
29	
30	
31	

Month /Year			
Monday	**Tuesday**	**Wednesday**	**Thursday**
1	1	1	1
2	2	2	2
3	3	3	3
4	4	4	4
5	5	5	5
Notes	**Notes**	**Notes**	**Notes**

Weekly motivation or goal:

Friday	Saturday	Sunday	Notes
1	1	1	
2	2	2	
3	3	3	
4	4	4	
5	5	5	
Notes	**Notes**	**Notes**	

Month /Year			
Monday	**Tuesday**	**Wednesday**	**Thursday**
1	1	1	1
2	2	2	2
3	3	3	3
4	4	4	4
5	5	5	5
Notes	Notes	Notes	Notes

Weekly motivation or goal:			
Friday	**Saturday**	**Sunday**	**Notes**
1	1	1	
2	2	2	
3	3	3	
4	4	4	
5	5	5	
Notes	**Notes**	**Notes**	

Month /Year			
Monday	**Tuesday**	**Wednesday**	**Thursday**
1	1	1	1
2	2	2	2
3	3	3	3
4	4	4	4
5	5	5	5
Notes	Notes	Notes	Notes

Weekly motivation or goal:

Friday	Saturday	Sunday	Notes
1	1	1	
2	2	2	
3	3	3	
4	4	4	
5	5	5	
Notes	Notes	Notes	

Month /Year

Monday	Tuesday	Wednesday	Thursday
1	1	1	1
2	2	2	2
3	3	3	3
4	4	4	4
5	5	5	5
Notes	Notes	Notes	Notes

Weekly motivation or goal:

Friday	Saturday	Sunday	Notes
1	1	1	
2	2	2	
3	3	3	
4	4	4	
5	5	5	
Notes	**Notes**	**Notes**	

Month /Year			
Monday	**Tuesday**	**Wednesday**	**Thursday**
1	1	1	1
2	2	2	2
3	3	3	3
4	4	4	4
5	5	5	5
Notes	**Notes**	**Notes**	**Notes**

Weekly motivation or goal:

Friday	Saturday	Sunday	Notes
1	1	1	
2	2	2	
3	3	3	
4	4	4	
5	5	5	
Notes	Notes	Notes	

Month

Year

Motivational quote / Monthly Goal

Month/Year			
Monday	**Tuesday**	**Wednesday**	**Thursday**
—	—	—	—
—	—	—	—
—	—	—	—
—	—	—	—
—	—	—	—

Motivation:			
Friday	**Saturday**	**Sunday**	**Notes**
—	—	—	—
—	—	—	—
—	—	—	—
—	—	—	—

Month/Year	
Important Dates	**Tasks**
1	
2	
3	
4	
5	
6	
7	
8	
9	
10	
11	
12	
13	
14	
15	
16	
17	
18	
19	
20	
21	
22	
23	
24	
25	
26	
27	
28	
29	
30	
31	

Month /Year			
Monday	**Tuesday**	**Wednesday**	**Thursday**
1	1	1	1
2	2	2	2
3	3	3	3
4	4	4	4
5	5	5	5
Notes	**Notes**	**Notes**	**Notes**

Weekly motivation or goal:

Friday	Saturday	Sunday	Notes
1	1	1	
2	2	2	
3	3	3	
4	4	4	
5	5	5	
Notes	**Notes**	**Notes**	

Month /Year			
Monday	**Tuesday**	**Wednesday**	**Thursday**
1	1	1	1
2	2	2	2
3	3	3	3
4	4	4	4
5	5	5	5
Notes	**Notes**	**Notes**	**Notes**

Weekly motivation or goal:

Friday	Saturday	Sunday	Notes
1	1	1	
2	2	2	
3	3	3	
4	4	4	
5	5	5	
Notes	**Notes**	**Notes**	

Month /Year			
Monday	**Tuesday**	**Wednesday**	**Thursday**
1	1	1	1
2	2	2	2
3	3	3	3
4	4	4	4
5	5	5	5
Notes	**Notes**	**Notes**	**Notes**

Weekly motivation or goal:

Friday	Saturday	Sunday	Notes
1	1	1	
2	2	2	
3	3	3	
4	4	4	
5	5	5	
Notes	**Notes**	**Notes**	

Month /Year			
Monday	**Tuesday**	**Wednesday**	**Thursday**
1	1	1	1
2	2	2	2
3	3	3	3
4	4	4	4
5	5	5	5
Notes	Notes	Notes	Notes

Weekly motivation or goal:

Friday	Saturday	Sunday	Notes
1	1	1	
2	2	2	
3	3	3	
4	4	4	
5	5	5	
Notes	**Notes**	**Notes**	

Month /Year			
Monday	**Tuesday**	**Wednesday**	**Thursday**
1	1	1	1
2	2	2	2
3	3	3	3
4	4	4	4
5	5	5	5
Notes	**Notes**	**Notes**	**Notes**

Weekly motivation or goal:

Friday	Saturday	Sunday	Notes
1	1	1	
2	2	2	
3	3	3	
4	4	4	
5	5	5	
Notes	**Notes**	**Notes**	

Month

Year

Motivational quote / Monthly Goal

Month/Year			
Monday	**Tuesday**	**Wednesday**	**Thursday**
—	—	—	—
—	—	—	—
—	—	—	—
—	—	—	—
—	—	—	—

Motivation:

Friday	Saturday	Sunday	Notes
—	—	—	—
—	—	—	—
—	—	—	—
—	—	—	—

Month/Year	
Important Dates	**Tasks**
1	
2	
3	
4	
5	
6	
7	
8	
9	
10	
11	
12	
13	
14	
15	
16	
17	
18	
19	
20	
21	
22	
23	
24	
25	
26	
27	
28	
29	
30	
31	

Month /Year

Monday	Tuesday	Wednesday	Thursday
1	1	1	1
2	2	2	2
3	3	3	3
4	4	4	4
5	5	5	5
Notes	**Notes**	**Notes**	**Notes**

Weekly motivation or goal:

Friday	Saturday	Sunday	Notes
1	1	1	
2	2	2	
3	3	3	
4	4	4	
5	5	5	
Notes	**Notes**	**Notes**	

Month /Year			
Monday	**Tuesday**	**Wednesday**	**Thursday**
1	1	1	1
2	2	2	2
3	3	3	3
4	4	4	4
5	5	5	5
Notes	Notes	Notes	Notes

Weekly motivation or goal:

Friday	Saturday	Sunday	Notes
1	1	1	
2	2	2	
3	3	3	
4	4	4	
5	5	5	
Notes	**Notes**	**Notes**	

Month /Year			
Monday	**Tuesday**	**Wednesday**	**Thursday**
1	1	1	1
2	2	2	2
3	3	3	3
4	4	4	4
5	5	5	5
Notes	**Notes**	**Notes**	**Notes**

Weekly motivation or goal:

Friday	Saturday	Sunday	Notes
1	1	1	
2	2	2	
3	3	3	
4	4	4	
5	5	5	
Notes	**Notes**	**Notes**	

Month /Year			
Monday	**Tuesday**	**Wednesday**	**Thursday**
1	1	1	1
2	2	2	2
3	3	3	3
4	4	4	4
5	5	5	5
Notes	Notes	Notes	Notes

Weekly motivation or goal:

Friday	Saturday	Sunday	Notes
1	1	1	
2	2	2	
3	3	3	
4	4	4	
5	5	5	
Notes	**Notes**	**Notes**	

Month /Year

Monday	Tuesday	Wednesday	Thursday
1	1	1	1
2	2	2	2
3	3	3	3
4	4	4	4
5	5	5	5
Notes	**Notes**	**Notes**	**Notes**

Weekly motivation or goal:

Friday	Saturday	Sunday	Notes
1	1	1	
2	2	2	
3	3	3	
4	4	4	
5	5	5	
Notes	**Notes**	**Notes**	

Month

Year

Motivational quote / Monthly Goal

Month/Year			
Monday	**Tuesday**	**Wednesday**	**Thursday**
—	—	—	—
—	—	—	—
—	—	—	—
—	—	—	—
—	—	—	—

Motivation:			
Friday	**Saturday**	**Sunday**	**Notes**
—	—	—	—
—	—	—	—
—	—	—	—
—	—	—	—

Month/Year	
Important Dates	**Tasks**
1	
2	
3	
4	
5	
6	
7	
8	
9	
10	
11	
12	
13	
14	
15	
16	
17	
18	
19	
20	
21	
22	
23	
24	
25	
26	
27	
28	
29	
30	
31	

Month /Year			
Monday	**Tuesday**	**Wednesday**	**Thursday**
1	1	1	1
2	2	2	2
3	3	3	3
4	4	4	4
5	5	5	5
Notes	Notes	Notes	Notes

Weekly motivation or goal:

Friday	Saturday	Sunday	Notes
1	1	1	
2	2	2	
3	3	3	
4	4	4	
5	5	5	
Notes	**Notes**	**Notes**	

Month /Year			
Monday	**Tuesday**	**Wednesday**	**Thursday**
1	**1**	**1**	**1**
2	**2**	**2**	**2**
3	**3**	**3**	**3**
4	**4**	**4**	**4**
5	**5**	**5**	**5**
Notes	**Notes**	**Notes**	**Notes**

Weekly motivation or goal:			
Friday	**Saturday**	**Sunday**	**Notes**
1	1	1	
2	2	2	
3	3	3	
4	4	4	
5	5	5	
Notes	**Notes**	**Notes**	

Month /Year			
Monday	**Tuesday**	**Wednesday**	**Thursday**
1	1	1	1
2	2	2	2
3	3	3	3
4	4	4	4
5	5	5	5
Notes	Notes	Notes	Notes

Weekly motivation or goal:

Friday	**Saturday**	**Sunday**	**Notes**
1	1	1	
2	2	2	
3	3	3	
4	4	4	
5	5	5	
Notes	**Notes**	**Notes**	

Month /Year			
Monday	**Tuesday**	**Wednesday**	**Thursday**
1	1	1	1
2	2	2	2
3	3	3	3
4	4	4	4
5	5	5	5
Notes	**Notes**	**Notes**	**Notes**

Weekly motivation or goal:

Friday	Saturday	Sunday	Notes
1	1	1	
2	2	2	
3	3	3	
4	4	4	
5	5	5	
Notes	**Notes**	**Notes**	

Month /Year			
Monday	**Tuesday**	**Wednesday**	**Thursday**
1	1	1	1
2	2	2	2
3	3	3	3
4	4	4	4
5	5	5	5
Notes	Notes	Notes	Notes

Weekly motivation or goal:			
Friday	**Saturday**	**Sunday**	**Notes**
1	1	1	
2	2	2	
3	3	3	
4	4	4	
5	5	5	
Notes	**Notes**	**Notes**	

Month

Year

Motivational quote / Monthly Goal

Month/Year

Monday	Tuesday	Wednesday	Thursday
—	—	—	—
—	—	—	—
—	—	—	—
—	—	—	—
—	—	—	—

Motivation:			
Friday	**Saturday**	**Sunday**	**Notes**
—	—	—	—
—	—	—	—
—	—	—	—
—	—	—	—

Month/Year	
Important Dates	**Tasks**
1	
2	
3	
4	
5	
6	
7	
8	
9	
10	
11	
12	
13	
14	
15	
16	
17	
18	
19	
20	
21	
22	
23	
24	
25	
26	
27	
28	
29	
30	
31	

Month /Year			
Monday	**Tuesday**	**Wednesday**	**Thursday**
1	1	1	1
2	2	2	2
3	3	3	3
4	4	4	4
5	5	5	5
Notes	Notes	Notes	Notes

Weekly motivation or goal:

Friday	Saturday	Sunday	Notes
1	1	1	
2	2	2	
3	3	3	
4	4	4	
5	5	5	
Notes	**Notes**	**Notes**	

Month /Year			
Monday	**Tuesday**	**Wednesday**	**Thursday**
1	1	1	1
2	2	2	2
3	3	3	3
4	4	4	4
5	5	5	5
Notes	Notes	Notes	Notes

Weekly motivation or goal:

Friday	Saturday	Sunday	Notes
1	1	1	
2	2	2	
3	3	3	
4	4	4	
5	5	5	
Notes	**Notes**	**Notes**	

Month /Year			
Monday	**Tuesday**	**Wednesday**	**Thursday**
1	1	1	1
2	2	2	2
3	3	3	3
4	4	4	4
5	5	5	5
Notes	Notes	Notes	Notes

Weekly motivation or goal:

Friday	Saturday	Sunday	Notes
1	1	1	
2	2	2	
3	3	3	
4	4	4	
5	5	5	
Notes	Notes	Notes	

Month /Year

Monday	Tuesday	Wednesday	Thursday
1	1	1	1
2	2	2	2
3	3	3	3
4	4	4	4
5	5	5	5
Notes	**Notes**	**Notes**	**Notes**

Weekly motivation or goal:			
Friday	**Saturday**	**Sunday**	**Notes**
1	1	1	
2	2	2	
3	3	3	
4	4	4	
5	5	5	
Notes	Notes	Notes	

Month /Year			
Monday	**Tuesday**	**Wednesday**	**Thursday**
1	1	1	1
2	2	2	2
3	3	3	3
4	4	4	4
5	5	5	5
Notes	**Notes**	**Notes**	**Notes**

Weekly motivation or goal:			
Friday	**Saturday**	**Sunday**	**Notes**
1	1	1	
2	2	2	
3	3	3	
4	4	4	
5	5	5	
Notes	**Notes**	**Notes**	

Month

Year

Motivational quote / Monthly Goal

Month/Year

Monday	Tuesday	Wednesday	Thursday
—	—	—	—
—	—	—	—
—	—	—	—
—	—	—	—
—	—	—	—

Motivation:

Friday	Saturday	Sunday	Notes
—	—	—	—
—	—	—	—
—	—	—	—
—	—	—	—

Month/Year	
Important Dates	**Tasks**
1	
2	
3	
4	
5	
6	
7	
8	
9	
10	
11	
12	
13	
14	
15	
16	
17	
18	
19	
20	
21	
22	
23	
24	
25	
26	
27	
28	
29	
30	
31	

Month /Year			
Monday	**Tuesday**	**Wednesday**	**Thursday**
1	1	1	1
2	2	2	2
3	3	3	3
4	4	4	4
5	5	5	5
Notes	**Notes**	**Notes**	**Notes**

Weekly motivation or goal:			
Friday	**Saturday**	**Sunday**	**Notes**
1	1	1	
2	2	2	
3	3	3	
4	4	4	
5	5	5	
Notes	**Notes**	**Notes**	

Month /Year

Monday	Tuesday	Wednesday	Thursday
1	1	1	1
2	2	2	2
3	3	3	3
4	4	4	4
5	5	5	5
Notes	**Notes**	**Notes**	**Notes**

Weekly motivation or goal:

Friday	Saturday	Sunday	Notes
1	1	1	
2	2	2	
3	3	3	
4	4	4	
5	5	5	
Notes	**Notes**	**Notes**	

Month /Year			
Monday	**Tuesday**	**Wednesday**	**Thursday**
1	1	1	1
2	2	2	2
3	3	3	3
4	4	4	4
5	5	5	5
Notes	Notes	Notes	Notes

Weekly motivation or goal:

Friday	Saturday	Sunday	Notes
1	1	1	
2	2	2	
3	3	3	
4	4	4	
5	5	5	
Notes	Notes	Notes	

Month /Year			
Monday	**Tuesday**	**Wednesday**	**Thursday**
1	1	1	1
2	2	2	2
3	3	3	3
4	4	4	4
5	5	5	5
Notes	Notes	Notes	Notes

Weekly motivation or goal:

Friday	Saturday	Sunday	Notes
1	1	1	
2	2	2	
3	3	3	
4	4	4	
5	5	5	
Notes	**Notes**	**Notes**	

Month /Year

Monday	Tuesday	Wednesday	Thursday
1	1	1	1
2	2	2	2
3	3	3	3
4	4	4	4
5	5	5	5
Notes	Notes	Notes	Notes

Weekly motivation or goal:			
Friday	**Saturday**	**Sunday**	**Notes**
1	1	1	
2	2	2	
3	3	3	
4	4	4	
5	5	5	
Notes	**Notes**	**Notes**	

Month

Year

Motivational quote / Monthly Goal

Month/Year			
Monday	**Tuesday**	**Wednesday**	**Thursday**
—	—	—	—
—	—	—	—
—	—	—	—
—	—	—	—
—	—	—	—

Motivation:

Friday	Saturday	Sunday	Notes
—	—	—	—
—	—	—	—
—	—	—	—
—	—	—	—

Month/Year	
Important Dates	**Tasks**
1	
2	
3	
4	
5	
6	
7	
8	
9	
10	
11	
12	
13	
14	
15	
16	
17	
18	
19	
20	
21	
22	
23	
24	
25	
26	
27	
28	
29	
30	
31	

Month /Year			
Monday	**Tuesday**	**Wednesday**	**Thursday**
1	1	1	1
2	2	2	2
3	3	3	3
4	4	4	4
5	5	5	5
Notes	**Notes**	**Notes**	**Notes**

Weekly motivation or goal:

Friday	Saturday	Sunday	Notes
1	1	1	
2	2	2	
3	3	3	
4	4	4	
5	5	5	
Notes	**Notes**	**Notes**	

Month /Year			
Monday	**Tuesday**	**Wednesday**	**Thursday**
1	1	1	1
2	2	2	2
3	3	3	3
4	4	4	4
5	5	5	5
Notes	**Notes**	**Notes**	**Notes**

Weekly motivation or goal:

Friday	Saturday	Sunday	Notes
1	1	1	
2	2	2	
3	3	3	
4	4	4	
5	5	5	
Notes	**Notes**	**Notes**	

Month /Year			
Monday	**Tuesday**	**Wednesday**	**Thursday**
1	1	1	1
2	2	2	2
3	3	3	3
4	4	4	4
5	5	5	5
Notes	**Notes**	**Notes**	**Notes**

Weekly motivation or goal:

Friday	Saturday	Sunday	Notes
1	1	1	
2	2	2	
3	3	3	
4	4	4	
5	5	5	
Notes	**Notes**	**Notes**	

Month /Year			
Monday	**Tuesday**	**Wednesday**	**Thursday**
1	1	1	1
2	2	2	2
3	3	3	3
4	4	4	4
5	5	5	5
Notes	Notes	Notes	Notes

Weekly motivation or goal:

Friday	Saturday	Sunday	Notes
1	1	1	
2	2	2	
3	3	3	
4	4	4	
5	5	5	
Notes	**Notes**	**Notes**	

Month /Year			
Monday	**Tuesday**	**Wednesday**	**Thursday**
1	1	1	1
2	2	2	2
3	3	3	3
4	4	4	4
5	5	5	5
Notes	**Notes**	**Notes**	**Notes**

Weekly motivation or goal:

Friday	Saturday	Sunday	Notes
1	1	1	
2	2	2	
3	3	3	
4	4	4	
5	5	5	
Notes	**Notes**	**Notes**	

Month

Year

Motivational quote / Monthly Goal

Month/Year

Monday	Tuesday	Wednesday	Thursday
—	—	—	—
—	—	—	—
—	—	—	—
—	—	—	—
—	—	—	—

Motivation:			
Friday	**Saturday**	**Sunday**	**Notes**
—	—	—	—
—	—	—	—
—	—	—	—
—	—	—	—

Month/Year	
Important Dates	**Tasks**
1	
2	
3	
4	
5	
6	
7	
8	
9	
10	
11	
12	
13	
14	
15	
16	
17	
18	
19	
20	
21	
22	
23	
24	
25	
26	
27	
28	
29	
30	
31	

Month /Year			
Monday	**Tuesday**	**Wednesday**	**Thursday**
1	1	1	1
2	2	2	2
3	3	3	3
4	4	4	4
5	5	5	5
Notes	**Notes**	**Notes**	**Notes**

Weekly motivation or goal:

Friday	Saturday	Sunday	Notes
1	1	1	
2	2	2	
3	3	3	
4	4	4	
5	5	5	
Notes	Notes	Notes	

Month /Year			
Monday	Tuesday	Wednesday	Thursday
1	1	1	1
2	2	2	2
3	3	3	3
4	4	4	4
5	5	5	5
Notes	Notes	Notes	Notes

Weekly motivation or goal:

Friday	Saturday	Sunday	Notes
1	1	1	
2	2	2	
3	3	3	
4	4	4	
5	5	5	
Notes	**Notes**	**Notes**	

Month /Year			
Monday	**Tuesday**	**Wednesday**	**Thursday**
1	1	1	1
2	2	2	2
3	3	3	3
4	4	4	4
5	5	5	5
Notes	**Notes**	**Notes**	**Notes**

Weekly motivation or goal:			
Friday	**Saturday**	**Sunday**	**Notes**
1	1	1	
2	2	2	
3	3	3	
4	4	4	
5	5	5	
Notes	**Notes**	**Notes**	

Month /Year			
Monday	**Tuesday**	**Wednesday**	**Thursday**
1	1	1	1
2	2	2	2
3	3	3	3
4	4	4	4
5	5	5	5
Notes	**Notes**	**Notes**	**Notes**

Weekly motivation or goal:

Friday	Saturday	Sunday	Notes
1	1	1	
2	2	2	
3	3	3	
4	4	4	
5	5	5	
Notes	**Notes**	**Notes**	

Month /Year			
Monday	**Tuesday**	**Wednesday**	**Thursday**
1	1	1	1
2	2	2	2
3	3	3	3
4	4	4	4
5	5	5	5
Notes	Notes	Notes	Notes

Weekly motivation or goal:

Friday	Saturday	Sunday	Notes
1	1	1	
2	2	2	
3	3	3	
4	4	4	
5	5	5	
Notes	**Notes**	**Notes**	

Month

Year

Motivational quote / Monthly Goal

Month/Year			
Monday	**Tuesday**	**Wednesday**	**Thursday**
—	—	—	—
—	—	—	—
—	—	—	—
—	—	—	—
—	—	—	—

Motivation:

Friday	Saturday	Sunday	Notes
—	—	—	—
—	—	—	—
—	—	—	—
—	—	—	—

Month/Year	
Important Dates	**Tasks**
1	
2	
3	
4	
5	
6	
7	
8	
9	
10	
11	
12	
13	
14	
15	
16	
17	
18	
19	
20	
21	
22	
23	
24	
25	
26	
27	
28	
29	
30	
31	

Month /Year			
Monday	**Tuesday**	**Wednesday**	**Thursday**
1	1	1	1
2	2	2	2
3	3	3	3
4	4	4	4
5	5	5	5
Notes	**Notes**	**Notes**	**Notes**

Weekly motivation or goal:

Friday	Saturday	Sunday	Notes
1	1	1	
2	2	2	
3	3	3	
4	4	4	
5	5	5	
Notes	**Notes**	**Notes**	

Month /Year			
Monday	**Tuesday**	**Wednesday**	**Thursday**
1	1	1	1
2	2	2	2
3	3	3	3
4	4	4	4
5	5	5	5
Notes	Notes	Notes	Notes

Weekly motivation or goal:

Friday	Saturday	Sunday	Notes
1	1	1	
2	2	2	
3	3	3	
4	4	4	
5	5	5	
Notes	**Notes**	**Notes**	

Month /Year			
Monday	**Tuesday**	**Wednesday**	**Thursday**
1	1	1	1
2	2	2	2
3	3	3	3
4	4	4	4
5	5	5	5
Notes	Notes	Notes	Notes

Weekly motivation or goal:

Friday	Saturday	Sunday	Notes
1	1	1	
2	2	2	
3	3	3	
4	4	4	
5	5	5	
Notes	**Notes**	**Notes**	

Month /Year			
Monday	**Tuesday**	**Wednesday**	**Thursday**
1	1	1	1
2	2	2	2
3	3	3	3
4	4	4	4
5	5	5	5
Notes	**Notes**	**Notes**	**Notes**

Weekly motivation or goal:

Friday	Saturday	Sunday	Notes
1	1	1	
2	2	2	
3	3	3	
4	4	4	
5	5	5	
Notes	Notes	Notes	

Month /Year			
Monday	**Tuesday**	**Wednesday**	**Thursday**
1	1	1	1
2	2	2	2
3	3	3	3
4	4	4	4
5	5	5	5
Notes	Notes	Notes	Notes

Weekly motivation or goal:

Friday	Saturday	Sunday	Notes
1	1	1	
2	2	2	
3	3	3	
4	4	4	
5	5	5	
Notes	**Notes**	**Notes**	

Month

Year

Motivational quote / Monthly Goal

Month/Year			
Monday	**Tuesday**	**Wednesday**	**Thursday**
—	—	—	—
—	—	—	—
—	—	—	—
—	—	—	—
—	—	—	—

Motivation:			
Friday	**Saturday**	**Sunday**	**Notes**
—	—	—	—
—	—	—	—
—	—	—	—
—	—	—	—

Month/Year	
Important Dates	**Tasks**
1	
2	
3	
4	
5	
6	
7	
8	
9	
10	
11	
12	
13	
14	
15	
16	
17	
18	
19	
20	
21	
22	
23	
24	
25	
26	
27	
28	
29	
30	
31	

Month /Year

Monday	Tuesday	Wednesday	Thursday
1	1	1	1
2	2	2	2
3	3	3	3
4	4	4	4
5	5	5	5
Notes	Notes	Notes	Notes

Weekly motivation or goal:

Friday	Saturday	Sunday	Notes
1	1	1	
2	2	2	
3	3	3	
4	4	4	
5	5	5	
Notes	**Notes**	**Notes**	

Month /Year			
Monday	Tuesday	Wednesday	Thursday
1	1	1	1
2	2	2	2
3	3	3	3
4	4	4	4
5	5	5	5
Notes	Notes	Notes	Notes

Weekly motivation or goal:

Friday	Saturday	Sunday	Notes
1	1	1	
2	2	2	
3	3	3	
4	4	4	
5	5	5	
Notes	**Notes**	**Notes**	

Month /Year			
Monday	**Tuesday**	**Wednesday**	**Thursday**
1	1	1	1
2	2	2	2
3	3	3	3
4	4	4	4
5	5	5	5
Notes	Notes	Notes	Notes

Weekly motivation or goal:

Friday	Saturday	Sunday	Notes
1	1	1	
2	2	2	
3	3	3	
4	4	4	
5	5	5	
Notes	**Notes**	**Notes**	

Month /Year

Monday	Tuesday	Wednesday	Thursday
1	1	1	1
2	2	2	2
3	3	3	3
4	4	4	4
5	5	5	5
Notes	**Notes**	**Notes**	**Notes**

Weekly motivation or goal:

Friday	Saturday	Sunday	Notes
1	1	1	
2	2	2	
3	3	3	
4	4	4	
5	5	5	
Notes	**Notes**	**Notes**	

Month /Year			
Monday	**Tuesday**	**Wednesday**	**Thursday**
1	1	1	1
2	2	2	2
3	3	3	3
4	4	4	4
5	5	5	5
Notes	Notes	Notes	Notes

Weekly motivation or goal:

Friday	Saturday	Sunday	Notes
1	1	1	
2	2	2	
3	3	3	
4	4	4	
5	5	5	
Notes	**Notes**	**Notes**	

Expenses

Expenses week of:				
Date	Description	Cash In	Cash Out	Bal

Expenses week of:

Date	Description	Cash In	Cash Out	Bal

Expenses week of:

Date	Description	Cash In	Cash Out	Bal

Expenses week of:

Date	Description	Cash In	Cash Out	Bal

Expenses week of:				
Date	**Description**	**Cash In**	**Cash Out**	**Bal**

Expenses week of:				
Date	Description	Cash In	Cash Out	Bal

Expenses week of:

Date	Description	Cash In	Cash Out	Bal

Expenses week of:

Date	Description	Cash In	Cash Out	Bal

Expenses week of:				
Date	**Description**	**Cash In**	**Cash Out**	**Bal**

Expenses week of:

Date	Description	Cash In	Cash Out	Bal

Expenses week of:

Date	Description	Cash In	Cash Out	Bal

Expenses week of:

Date	Description	Cash In	Cash Out	Bal

Expenses week of:

Date	Description	Cash In	Cash Out	Bal

Expenses week of:

Date	Description	Cash In	Cash Out	Bal

Expenses week of:

Date	Description	Cash In	Cash Out	Bal

Expenses week of:

Date	Description	Cash In	Cash Out	Bal

Expenses week of:

Date	Description	Cash In	Cash Out	Bal

Expenses week of:				
Date	Description	Cash In	Cash Out	Bal

Expenses week of:

Date	Description	Cash In	Cash Out	Bal

Expenses week of:				
Date	**Description**	**Cash In**	**Cash Out**	**Bal**

Expenses week of:

Date	Description	Cash In	Cash Out	Bal

Expenses week of:

Date	Description	Cash In	Cash Out	Bal

Expenses week of:

Date	Description	Cash In	Cash Out	Bal

Expenses week of:

Date	Description	Cash In	Cash Out	Bal

Expenses week of:

Date	Description	Cash In	Cash Out	Bal

Expenses week of:				
Date	Description	Cash In	Cash Out	Bal

Expenses week of:				
Date	**Description**	**Cash In**	**Cash Out**	**Bal**

Expenses week of:

Date	Description	Cash In	Cash Out	Bal

Expenses week of:

Date	Description	Cash In	Cash Out	Bal

Expenses week of:

Date	Description	Cash In	Cash Out	Bal

Expenses week of:

Date	Description	Cash In	Cash Out	Bal

Expenses week of:				
Date	Description	Cash In	Cash Out	Bal

Expenses week of:

Date	Description	Cash In	Cash Out	Bal

Expenses week of:

Date	Description	Cash In	Cash Out	Bal

Expenses week of:

Date	Description	Cash In	Cash Out	Bal

Expenses week of:

Date	Description	Cash In	Cash Out	Bal

Expenses week of:

Date	Description	Cash In	Cash Out	Bal

Expenses week of:

Date	Description	Cash In	Cash Out	Bal

Expenses week of:

Date	Description	Cash In	Cash Out	Bal

Expenses week of:

Date	Description	Cash In	Cash Out	Bal

Expenses week of:

Date	Description	Cash In	Cash Out	Bal

Expenses week of:

Date	Description	Cash In	Cash Out	Bal

Expenses week of:				
Date	**Description**	**Cash In**	**Cash Out**	**Bal**

Expenses week of:

Date	Description	Cash In	Cash Out	Bal

Expenses week of:

Date	Description	Cash In	Cash Out	Bal

Expenses week of:

Date	Description	Cash In	Cash Out	Bal

Expenses week of:

Date	Description	Cash In	Cash Out	Bal

Expenses week of:

Date	Description	Cash In	Cash Out	Bal

Expenses week of:

Date	Description	Cash In	Cash Out	Bal

Expenses week of:

Date	Description	Cash In	Cash Out	Bal

Expenses week of:

Date	Description	Cash In	Cash Out	Bal

Expenses week of:

Date	Description	Cash In	Cash Out	Bal

Expenses week of:

Date	Description	Cash In	Cash Out	Bal

Notes

Index

Page	Index	Page	Index

Page	Index	Page	Index

Page	Index	Page	Index

Page	Index	Page	Index

Page	Index	Page	Index

Page	Index	Page	Index

Page	Index	Page	Index

Page	Index	Page	Index

Page	Index	Page	Index